CHANGING TIMES
ANCIENT GREECE

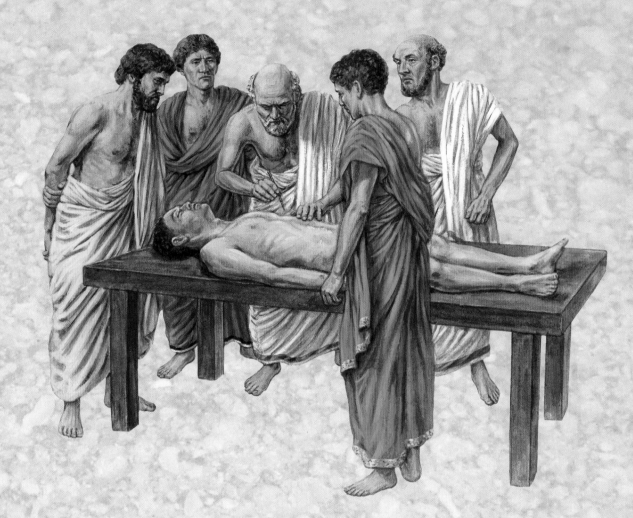

Health and Disease

By Richard Dargie

Illustrated by Adam Hook

First published in 2007 by
Compass Point Books
3109 West 50th Street, #115
Minneapolis, MN 55410
Visit Compass Point Books on the Internet at *www.compasspointbooks.com*
or e-mail your request to *custserv@compasspointbooks.com*

Library of Congress Cataloging-in-Publication Data
Dargie, Richard.
　Ancient Greece health and disease / by Richard Dargie ; illustrations by Adam Hook.
　　p. cm. -- (Changing times)
　Includes bibliographical references and index.
　ISBN-13: 978-0-7565-2087-8 (library binding)
　ISBN-10: 0-7565-2087-8 (library binding)
1. Medicine, Greek and Roman. I. Hook, Adam. II. Title. III. Series.

　R138.D37 2006
　610.938--dc22

2006027043

Image Credits
AKG: 12 (John Hios). Art Archive: 6 (Cyprus Museum, Nicosia/Dagli Orti), 9 (Archaeological Museum, Piraeus/Dagli Orti), 10 (Anagni Cathedral, Italy/Dagli Orti [A]), 17 (National Archaeological Museum, Athens/Dagli Orti), 19, 25 (Dagli Orti), 27 (Museo della Civilta Romana, Rome/Dagli Orti).Bridgeman Art Library: 21 (British Museum, London), 29 (Louvre, Paris). Wellcome Trust Library: 14, 22.

Contents

Introduction   4

Early Ideas About Disease   6

Gods Who Healed   8

Understanding the Body   10

Common Complaints   12

Greek Doctors   14

Doctors' Diagnoses   16

Drugs and Herbs   18

Healthy Lifestyle   20

Pregnancy and Birth   22

Epidemics   24

Wounds and Operations   26

Mental Illness   28

Timeline   30

Glossary and Further Information   31

Index   32

Introduction

Who Were the Ancient Greeks?

The ancient Greeks were a remarkable people who helped lay the foundations of our civilization. They lived in what is now Greece, on the surrounding Mediterranean islands, and on the neighboring coast of Asia Minor.

Ancient Greek civilization began on the island of Crete in about 2000 B.C. Spreading to the mainland, it reached its height during the Classical Period (480–330 B.C.). It lost political independence in about 150 B.C. to the Roman empire but played a major role in shaping Roman life.

The ancient Greeks lived in small, independent city-states. Each one consisted of a city and its surrounding farmland. The most powerful city-states were Attica (Athens) and Laconia (Sparta), a tough soldier-state. The Athenians were rich traders whose influence extended across the Mediterranean Sea. Their city was also a center for the arts and learning. It was home to some of the finest thinkers, writers, and artists the world has ever seen. The Athenians wrote and performed the first plays and developed the idea of democratic government. It is largely because of them that we remember the ancient Greeks today.

Health and Disease in Ancient Greece

Ordinary Greeks thought illness was caused by the gods and they used magic and charms as cures. The Greeks worshipped many gods. They believed the god Asklepios was responsible for medicine and healing. Many ancient Greeks prayed to Asklepios or other gods to cure them of sickness or injury.

Not everyone believed the gods were responsible for everything. Greek philosophers spent a lot of time trying to understand the world, including the workings of the human body. They came up with scientific explanations for diseases.

The Greeks left behind detailed descriptions of the illnesses people suffered. Greek doctors believed they should observe their patients and carefully record what they saw. The most famous Greek doctor was Hippocrates (460–380 B.C.). The *Hippocratic Corpus* is a collection of about 60 writings on medicine, all under Hippocrates' name but actually written by many people. The writings reject superstition and look to science to explain disease.

Early Ideas About Disease

Before the days of science, people used stories about gods and heroes to explain the world, including the mysteries of health and disease. One of the earliest stories that survives from ancient Greece is *The Iliad*, composed by the poet Homer around 800 B.C. It tells of the siege of Ilion (Troy). *Works and Days*, written by Hesiod about 100 years later, contains myths about the Greek gods. These writings are not just stories. They reveal how the early Greeks believed that the gods influenced their lives.

The statue of Zeus, king of all the Greek gods, dates back to 500 B.C.

> *[Apollo] attacked the mules first and the swift dogs, but then he loosed his piercing shafts upon the men themselves.*
>
> HOMER, *THE ILIAD*

shafts: arrows

At the beginning of *The Iliad*, the Greek army surrounds the city of Troy. The sun god Apollo fires arrows at the Greeks, which brings a terrible nine-day plague. Rather than understanding that there could be a natural cause for the plague—such as the poor living conditions in the army camp—Homer explains the plague as a punishment caused by one of the gods. According to the story, Apollo was angry about the way Agamemnon, one of the Greek princes, had treated his priest Chryses.

and by night ...

continually by day

for the earth is full of evils and the sea is full.

> *Countless plagues wander among men; for the earth is full of evils and the sea is full. Diseases spontaneously come upon men continually by day and by night ...*
> HESIOD, WORKS AND DAYS

spontaneously: with no obvious cause

One Greek story tells how a woman named Pandora let disease escape into the world. The only thing that did not escape from the jar was Hope.

In this part of *Works and Days*, Hesiod describes what happened, according to Greek myth, after Pandora's box was opened. The story of Pandora is an early fable that tries to explain how disease came into the world. Zeus, the king of the gods, made Pandora. She owned a box or jar that contained all evils and disease. Out of curiosity, she opened the jar, even though she had been warned not to. When she did so, all diseases escaped.

Gods Who Healed

As well as thinking the gods were responsible for disease, the early Greeks also believed the gods had the power to cure. When people were sick or injured, they prayed to one of the gods, offered up sacrifices, and sometimes took part in healing ceremonies at home or at a temple. An *asklepieion* was a temple dedicated to Asklepios, the god of medicine. Other gods associated with healing included Apollo, the sun god; Panacea, the goddess of herbal healing; and Hygeia, the goddess of health.

Straightaway [Apollo] made his pains cease and staunched the black blood that flowed from his grievous wound and put strength in his heart.

HOMER, THE ILIAD

staunched: stopped
grievous: serious

In the story of the Trojan War, the Greek hero Glaucus is wounded by an arrow. Glaucus prays to the god Apollo, who heals him and makes him strong again. Prayers were usually accompanied by gifts to the gods. Sometimes people paid a priest to sacrifice an animal, usually a sheep or an ox. The animal would be killed and then burned over a fire. People also made offerings of gold or silver coins, flasks of wine or olive oil, or whatever they could afford.

A Greek priest prepared to sacrifice an ox. The Greeks believed offerings like this kept the gods happy.

*A votive relief shows the god Asklepios treating a sleeping woman.
He is attended by the goddess of health, Hygeia.*

*Asklepios cut open his belly, excised the
abscess, [and] sewed him up again.*
VOTIVE COLUMN AT EPIDAURUS

excised: cut out
abscess: pus-filled sore

A votive relief is a stone inscribed with thanks to one of the gods. Many votive columns were left for the god Asklepios at Epidaurus, the site of the largest shrine. Sick people visited such holy places hoping to be cured. They often stayed overnight. Some believed the god visited them and cured them as they slept—more likely, priests performed secret surgeries. Priests also interpreted patients' dreams to identify their illness and provide a treatment. Treatments included herbal remedies, special diets, and exercises.

9

Understanding the Body

By about 400 B.C., the Greeks had begun to develop a science of medicine. Hippocrates had a theory that the body was made up of four humors: black bile, yellow bile, phlegm, and blood. He believed these were linked to the four elements that made up the universe: earth, fire, water, and air. Although the theory of humors was wrong, it was still a great leap forward. It was the first time people had looked for natural causes for disease instead of blaming gods or spirits.

The Greek idea of the four humors was still accepted in Europe as late as the Middle Ages, as seen in a 13th-century fresco.

There are four forms from which the body is composed, earth, fire, water, air, and disorders and diseases arise from the unnatural excess or deficiency of these.

PLATO, *TIMAEUS*

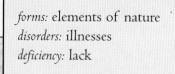

forms: elements of nature
disorders: illnesses
deficiency: lack

Talking here to the Greek thinker Socrates, the character Timaeus describes the four elements that make up the body. This was another way of talking about the four humors. The Greeks believed the elements or humors had to be in balance and that having too much or too little of one caused disease. The Greeks came up with treatments for diseases based on this theory. For example, problems caused by excess blood, such as having a headache or fever, were treated by bloodletting.

A Greek doctor prepares to cut open a human body at a medical school in Alexandria.

[T]o cut open the bodies of the dead is necessary for medical students. For they ought to know the position and arrangement of its parts.

CORNELIUS CELSUS,
ON MEDICINE

The Greeks created a detailed picture of human anatomy. They learned from the ancient Egyptian process of embalming (preserving dead bodies). Human dissection took place in medical schools at Alexandria from the 200s B.C. Students cut open and examined human bodies, usually of criminals, who were sometimes still alive. Later it was forbidden, but students performed vivisection—cutting open live animals, including apes, pigs, and dogs. Vivisection helped the Greeks to understand how the heart pumped blood and how the lungs took in air.

Common Complaints

Many of the illnesses suffered by the ancient Greeks are still around today. In his writings, Hippocrates described a range of complaints, including asthma, pneumonia, and cholera. Hippocrates thought certain diseases were more likely depending on the age of the patient, the time of year, or even where the patient lived. For example, he thought people who lived in cities that were sheltered from the north were more likely to suffer epilepsy. The healthiest place to live was thought to be Athens, the center of the Greek world.

> *Old men suffer from difficulty in breathing, ... painful joints, nephritis, dizziness, ... sleeplessness, ... dim-sightedness, blindness from glaucoma, hardness of hearing.*
>
> HIPPOCRATES, *APHORISMS*

nephritis: kidney disease
glaucoma: eye disorder

Some ancient Greeks suffered from varicose (swollen) veins, a complaint still common today. This votive tablet thanks the god Asklepios for healing them.

Here Hippocrates lists the diseases that were most likely suffered by the elderly, such as poor eyesight and hearing. In the same work, he lists diseases of babies, such as vomiting, teething, coughs, diarrhea, swollen navels, and discharges from the ears. Hippocrates said problems such as tonsillitis, asthma, worms, and nosebleeds were common in older children. Pleurisy, pneumonia, and hemorrhoids were some of the complaints of adult life.

painful joints, nephritis, dizziness, ... sleeplessness, ... dim-sightedness,

> *All diseases occur at all seasons, but some occur more frequently and with greater severity at certain seasons.*
>
> HIPPOCRATES, *APHORISMS*

severity: seriousness, harshness

Like us, the Greeks were more likely to get coughs, colds, sore throats, and pneumonia in winter. Summer was a time when more people suffered from prickly heat, fever, vomiting, and diarrhea. Such complaints were caused by being out in the sun or by eating food that had spoiled in the heat. However, doctors such as Hippocrates began to link certain diseases with the different seasons. They said dysentery, tuberculosis, and hip disease were more common in the fall, while spring could bring mental illness, epilepsy, and a skin disease called psoriasis.

When explaining disease, Greek doctors looked for natural causes. Winter weather could bring colds and flu.

blindness from glaucoma, hardness of hearing.

Greek Doctors

Surgeons and pharmacists played a part in treating disease, but doctors were the medical experts. The best Greek doctors devoted their lives to healing the sick. They visited their patients often and tried to have a kind bedside manner. They were very careful about how they behaved because they didn't want to give doctors a bad name. Hippocrates wrote down lots of advice to doctors and a promise for all doctors to make—the Hippocratic oath. Even today, doctors take a modern version of the Hippocratic oath.

A fragment of papyrus from the third century B.C. was inscribed with the Hippocratic oath (the promise made by Greek doctors).

I will use treatments for the benefit of the sick to the best of my ability and judgment; I will abstain from doing harm.

THE HIPPOCRATIC OATH

abstain from: not do

The most important part of the Hippocratic oath was promising to do the very best for patients and to never cause them harm. Every doctor also swore never to give a patient poison, to keep all the information about patients a secret, and to teach other doctors. In other works, Hippocrates told doctors how to talk to their patients in a reassuring way.

abstain from doing harm.

> *The authority of a physician requires that he is of healthy complexion and plump as nature intended.*
>
> HIPPOCRATES, *PHYSICIAN*

complexion: quality of the skin

Hippocrates believed it was very important for doctors to look healthy. People would not believe a doctor could take care of them, he argued, if the doctor did not maintain an appropriate appearance. Greek doctors tried to follow a healthy lifestyle and to be clean and well-dressed. Hippocrates even suggested they should wear perfume to help lift the spirits of the sick. When they spoke to their patients, doctors were told to be calm and cheerful but never too friendly.

A Greek doctor gently examines a young patient.

Doctors' Diagnoses

Diagnosis means discovering what illness a patient is suffering from. Greek doctors reached a diagnosis by watching and examining their patients carefully. By keeping notes of what they saw, they could spot patterns or changes and learn how diseases developed. They believed the causes of disease fell into two main categories. Diseases could be caused by disturbances inside the patient—imbalances in the patient's humors—or by outside influences, such as the climate.

Theophrastus, a pupil of the philosopher Aristotle, believed a patient's tongue revealed his or her condition.

> [T]he majority of the symptoms displayed by those who are ill are found in the tongue.
>
> THEOPHRASTUS, *ON THE SENSES*

symptoms: signs (of an illness)

The examinations performed by Greek doctors might surprise us today. The scientist Theophrastus (372?–287? B.C.) suggested that doctors could learn almost everything they needed to know by examining a patient's tongue. This theory had first been introduced about a century earlier by a philosopher named Diogenes of Apollonia. Diogenes thought all the blood vessels in the body led to the tongue. Doctors also studied patients' dreams to help understand physical symptoms.

do no harm.

habit of two things—help, or at least

A carving from about 400 B.C. shows a patient being treated by the Greek physician Amphiaraos. The snake on the patient in bed is a symbol of the god Asklepios.

> *Declare the past, diagnose the present, foretell the future: practice these things. In diseases make a habit of two things—help, or at least do no harm.*
>
> HIPPOCRATES, *EPIDEMICS*

diagnose: analyze

Hippocrates describes the proper scientific method for caring for the sick. Greek doctors relied on prognosis—identifying the disease and predicting how it would develop. To reach their diagnosis, they had to "declare the past" or find out about symptoms. Once they knew what the disease was, they suggested treatments that would put the whole body back into balance. Some doctors specialized in natural healing—treatments such as diet, baths, massage, and exercise. Other doctors prescribed drugs and ointments as well.

Drugs and Herbs

The Greeks were knowledgeable about plants and their use as medicines. Root cutters made a living from collecting medicinal plants and often performed special rituals as they dug them up. Herbalists used the plants to prepare herbal remedies, which were often sold as magic cures. Doctors consulted herbals (books about medicinal plants) and mixed their own medicines. They even knew how to extract opium from poppies, which they used to relieve pain.

An ancient Greek herbalist ground up some fresh leaves to make a paste.

Herophilus, who was once held to be among the greatest physicians, is held to have said that drugs are the hands of the gods ... what divine touch can effect, drugs tested by use and experience also accomplish.
MARCELLUS, *LETTER OF CORNELIUS CELSUS ON REMEDIES*

Like many Greek doctors, Herophilus used tried and tested drugs to treat his patients. He thought drugs were so effective, it was as though they came from the gods themselves. Not all cures relied on drugs. When Herophilus saw patients with tuberculosis, he just changed their diet. Some Greeks did not approve of using drugs. Plato thought diseases had a set life span and that giving drugs upset the natural balance of things.

experience also accomplish.

touch can effect, drugs tested by use and

> *Fresh leaves of this plant when applied as a plaster with barley are good for inflammations of the eyes and those upon ulcers. It disperses all hardness and abscesses, glandular swellings, and tumors.*
>
> DIOSCORIDES,
> ON MEDICAL MATERIALS

inflammations: swellings

Mandrake is a poisonous plant from the nightshade family. It was thought to have magical properties because its roots can look like human figures. The Greeks used mandrake as an anesthetic (to stop a patient from feeling pain) and as a treatment for depression, fever, and even snakebites. Black hellebore (a flowering evergreen plant) also had many medicinal uses. Herbalists used the leaves, flowers, stems, or roots of plants and prepared them as potions, pastes, or powders.

Anethum graveolens.

Known as anethon *to the Greeks, dill had many uses. Chopped dill was stirred into gruel, a thin hot cereal, and eaten to help settle upset stomachs.*

Healthy Lifestyle

The ancient Greeks paid attention to their lifestyles. They understood that food and exercise affected health. The physician Diocles recommended walks before meals to increase the appetite and improve digestion. Sports were a regular part of life. The Greeks held games, such as the Olympics, where young athletes showed off their skills. Rich Greeks took spa baths and had massages to help them relax and to improve their circulation. Manual labor kept ordinary Greeks fit but also placed stress on their joints.

Wealthy people reclined on couches to eat and drink. Their diet included fish, meat from farm animals, and game.

And a carver lifted and placed by them platters of diverse kinds of flesh.
HOMER, *THE ODYSSEY*

platters: large plates
diverse kinds of flesh: different meats

Here the poet Homer describes a banquet for the hero Odysseus and his men. Meat was a luxury reserved for the rich who feasted on sheep, goat, pig, ox, hare, boar, and deer. Most ordinary Greeks ate fresh fruits, vegetables, fish, shellfish, and bread. People ate plenty of garlic, which is now believed to have many benefits, from fighting colds to preventing heart disease. They also enjoyed honey, which is known to help throat infections.

But there are many benefits which the enthusiastic sportsman may expect to derive from this pursuit. I speak of the health which will thereby accrue to the physical frame, the quickening of the eye and ear, the defiance of old age, and last, but not least, the warlike training which it ensures.

XENOPHON,
THE SPORTSMAN

accrue to: build up

The Greek historian Xenophon is describing why hunting with hounds was good for you. Then, as now, people realized physical exercise improved mood and well-being in addition to keeping the body in shape. The Greeks prized a good physique. Young men visited wrestling schools and gyms to keep fit and socialize, but women usually stayed home and did not exercise. The exception was women from the city-state of Sparta. They exercised even when they were pregnant, believing that this would help them have babies who would become great soldiers.

A bronze figurine features a young Spartan woman running. Sparta was unique in encouraging its women to exercise.

21

Pregnancy and Birth

Spartan girls married at 18, but in most of the Greek world, brides were 14 years old. The Greeks believed a young woman should become pregnant soon after puberty; otherwise, her womb might wander inside her body and cause illness. Pregnant women took herbs to start labor and to ease labor pains. They also used herbs to prevent pregnancy or abort unwanted babies. Pregnancy could be dangerous. Many Greek women died in childbirth, and the average female life span was only 34 years.

[The child] must necessarily resemble each parent in some respect, seeing that the seed comes from both parents to form the child.

HIPPOCRATES, ON GENERATION

The Greeks understood that both parents played a role in producing a baby. They used the word *seed* to describe what the father and mother contributed to the baby—today, we would refer to the genes inside the sperm and egg. The Greeks believed that seed came from every part of each parent's body and determined what each part of the child's body would look like. If the baby had ears like its mother's, for example, this meant the mother had contributed more seed from her ears than the father had from his.

A carved stone, or stele, was made in the sixth century B.C. for the tomb of a woman who died in childbirth.

Difficult labor occurs because a woman has had many troublesome pregnancies, for example three to five.

HEROPHILUS, *MIDWIFERY*

labor: the process of giving birth

Greek writings on childbirth were by men, such as the anatomist Herophilus, but men were not usually present at births. Women gave birth at home, attended by a midwife and a doula, a household slave. Midwives were women past their own childbearing years who had some medical training. After the birth, the mother was looked after by the midwife and other women for a few days. The father decided whether the family could keep the baby. In poorer families, where the parents would not be able to afford a girl's dowry (money or property given by a woman's family to her husband when she gets married), female babies were often abandoned.

When giving birth, Greek women were assisted by midwives or female members of their family.

parent in some respect, seeing that the seed comes from

Epidemics

As Greek cities grew and became more crowded, they became more likely to suffer epidemics—diseases that could sweep through a population, claiming many lives. The first known epidemic in ancient Greece struck Athens in 430 B.C. The historian Thucydides called the epidemic a plague, but it was probably smallpox, measles, or typhus. It even killed the leader of Athens, the great statesman Pericles. The same disease hit the city again four years later.

The epidemic that struck Athens in 430 B.C. took many lives. According to Thucydides, it killed a quarter of the population.

[I]t ravaged Athens most of all, then the other most populous places. Such was the history of the plague.
THUCYDIDES, *HISTORY OF THE PELOPONNESIAN WAR*

populous: densely populated

Thucydides included a detailed description of the Athenian plague in his history of the war between Athens and Sparta. The first signs of illness were red, swollen eyes, throat, and tongue. Next the victims had fits of sneezing, coughing, and retching. Their bodies became covered in blisters and sores, and they felt feverish and thirsty. Most died after about a week. Some survived but then had terrible diarrhea and died of exhaustion. A few victims did recover but lost body parts, such as their fingers, toes, or eyes.

> *Boys, young men and men in their prime were afflicted— mainly those who frequented the wrestling school and the gymnasia.*
>
> HIPPOCRATES, *EPIDEMICS*

afflicted: affected

Hippocrates left behind a whole treatise on epidemics. Here he describes what was probably an outbreak of mumps in Athens—the symptoms included spongy swellings on the body, hoarse coughs, and sometimes painful swelling of the testicles. It is not clear whether the Greeks understood about contagious diseases (diseases passed on through contact). Some think Hippocrates did understand mumps was contagious and that is why he described how it spread in public places. In other Hippocratic writings, epidemics are said to occur because everyone breathes the same bad air.

Wrestling schools, or palaestrae, were common throughout Greece. Pillars are all that remain of the one at Olympia.

Wounds and Operations

Early Greeks believed the god Asklepios operated on visitors to his shrine. In one story, a man visited the shrine with a stomach abscess and dreamed Asklepios cut out the abscess. The next morning, the floor was covered in blood. It is probable that priests at the shrine performed the operation. Greek surgeons learned to perform a range of operations, but surgery was risky. Although they used herbs to clot blood and heal wounds, surgeons had no knowledge of germs. Many patients died of infection.

Surgery was common on the battlefield, where surgeons routinely cut out spear tips and arrowheads.

Then ... the wound of the noble god-like Odysseus they bound skillfully and checked the dark blood with an incantation.

HOMER, *THE ODYSSEY*

incantation: singing, chanting

In this part of *The Odyssey*, the hero Odysseus has been gashed in the thigh by a wild boar. His cousins chant as they bandage the wound, which shows they are relying on magic and superstition. In *The Iliad*, Homer describes more practical medicine, as soldiers perform surgery on the battlefield. But the use of charms and chants continued among ordinary people long after the development of scientific medicine. They accompanied simple procedures such as binding wounds, applying plasters, or cutting out arrowheads.

is cut off, there is great danger of the

[I]f the patient suffers
pain during the amputation
and the limb happens to be
not yet dead at the place
where it is cut off, there is
great danger of the patient
fainting from pain.

HIPPOCRATES, *ON JOINTS*

amputation: cutting off

A carving shows a case of surgical instruments between two cupping glasses, which would have been used in bloodletting.

Hippocrates describes surgical treatment for a range of conditions, including, here, gangrene. He even lists what should be in the operating room—instruments, lights, assistants, and, of course, the surgeon and patient! Greek surgical tools included knives, saws, awls, drills, clamps, and pliers. The spoon of Diocles was specially designed for extracting a broad arrowhead or spear tip. Later doctors performed very advanced surgery. The physician Erasistratus is said to have opened up a patient's belly to treat swollen liver tissue.

Mental Illness

Like physical illness, mental illness was first believed to be caused by the gods. Dionysus, the god of wine, was thought to drive his followers into a mad frenzy. Other Greek myths describe the king of the gods, Zeus, or his wife, Hera, making people insane with grief or rage. From the time of Hippocrates, however, people began to look for a more scientific explanation of mental illness. Hippocrates said mental illness was caused by imbalances of the humors.

The Greeks recognized depression as an illness and called it melancholy. Sufferers gradually lost their will to live.

The patients are dull or stern, dejected or unreasonably torpid, without any manifest cause ... they also become peevish, dispirited, sleepless, and start up from a disturbed sleep.

ARETAEUS THE CAPPADOCIAN, *ON THE CAUSES AND SYMPTOMS OF CHRONIC DISEASE*

torpid: slow, sluggish

Here the physician Aretaeus describes the late stages of melancholy, which was, according to the Greeks, one of the two types of mental illness. Melancholy was similar to what is today called depression. Its first sign was poor spirits, but ultimately sufferers could be driven to suicide. The other type of mental illness was mania. Manic people were frenzied and wild. They might even commit murder. Melancholy was said to be caused by too much black bile, and mania by too much yellow bile.

fancying himself a brick, and fearing lest he should be dissolved.

given to extraordinary fantasies; for one ... will not drink, as

In the uneducated, the common employments are the carrying of loads, and working at clay ... they are also given to extraordinary fantasies; for one ... will not drink, as fancying himself a brick, and fearing lest he should be dissolved.

ARETAEUS THE CAPPADOCIAN,
ON THE CAUSES AND SYMPTOMS OF CHRONIC DISEASE

According to Aretaeus, patients with melancholy also suffered from delusions—imagining things that were not real or true—that left them in a state of constant fear. Aretaeus said some melancholic people believed they were birds, vases, or even gods. Some were even afraid to urinate because they thought they might flood the whole world. Those who suffered from mania, the other form of mental illness, were aggressive rather than fearful.

On a cup, Dionysus, god of wine, dances with his crazed female followers, the maenads.

29

Timeline

B.C.

c. 800   Homer's *The Iliad* and *The Odyssey* describe how the gods cause and cure disease.

c. 700   Hesiod's *Works and Days* describes how Zeus let disease into the world through Pandora's box.

500s   The earliest reference to a shrine to Asklepios at the seaport of Epidaurus.

c. 522   The Greek physician and prisoner of war Democedes practices medicine in the court of the Persian king, Darius I.

c. 500   Philosopher-scientist Alcmaeon dissects human bodies and discovers eustachian tubes in the ear.

c. 460   Hippocrates is born on the island of Kos.

c. 460   Diogenes of Apollonia writes detailed descriptions of blood vessels.

c. 430   Death of Empedocles, the philosopher who described the four humors.

c. 430   The first treatises of the *Hippocratic Corpus* are written.

430   An epidemic kills tens of thousands of Athenians.

c. 428   Birth of the philosopher Plato.

426   Another epidemic strikes Athens.

c. 380   Hippocrates dies.

c. 347   Death of the philosopher Plato.

c. 340   Praxagoras of Kos discovers the difference between arteries and veins.

c. 330   Greek physicians with Alexander the Great in India encounter ayurvedic medicine (medicine based on Hindu texts called the Vedas, written about 1000 B.C.).

c. 300   Death of Diocles of Carystus, who probably wrote the first herbal as well as treatises on other aspects of medicine, such as anatomy.

c. 300   Herophilus founds a school of anatomy at Alexandria, performs public dissections, and investigates the brain, digestive system, reproductive organs, and blood.

c. 265   The Romans come into contact with Greek medicine through prisoners of war.

c. 250   Erasistratus, who also founds a school of anatomy at Alexandria, distinguishes between types of nerves, and traces veins and arteries to the heart.

219   The Greek doctor Archagathus settles in Rome and establishes himself as a wound specialist.

c. 100   Heracleides of Tarentum investigates the painkilling properties of opium.

c. 90   The physician Asclepiades establishes Greek medicine in Rome, promoting natural healing (diet, massage, and exercise).

46   The Roman dictator Julius Caesar announces that all who practice medicine in Rome will be given the status of citizens.

A.D.

50   The Roman writer Celsus writes *On Medicine*, an encyclopedia of all Greek and Roman medical knowledge.

50–70   Dioscorides writes *De Materia Medica*, a five-book guide to drugs.

129   Galen is born at Pergamum, Asia Minor.

c. 150   Aretaeus of Cappadocia, who practices medicine in Rome and Alexandria, describes and names diabetes.

161   Galen becomes physician to Emperor Marcus Aurelius in Rome.

c. 200   Completion of the *Hippocratic Corpus*.

Glossary

Difficult words from the quoted material appear beside each quotation panel. This glossary explains words used in the main text.

abscess   A pus-filled area of swollen, infected tissue.
anesthetic   Something that stops a patient from feeling pain.
asthma   A condition that makes it difficult for a person to breathe.
bile   Bitter liquid made by the liver.
bloodletting   Cutting a vein, usually in the arm, to draw out blood.
cholera   A stomach infection that causes diarrhea.
contagious   Describes a disease that can be passed on through direct or indirect contact.
dissection   Cutting open a dead body in order to examine its parts.
dysentery   An infectious disease that causes severe diarrhea.
epidemic   A disease outbreak spreading rapidly across a population.
epilepsy   A condition of the nervous system that can cause seizures or fits.
genes   Instructions coded in the molecules of the cells in the human body.
glaucoma   An eye disease that can cause loss of sight.
hemorrhoids   Painful swollen tissue around the anus.
herbal remedy   A medicine made out of plants thought to have healing properties.
humor   Bodily fluid.
mania   One of the two categories of mental illness, according to the ancient Greeks, with symptoms of overexcitement and aggression.
melancholy   One of the two categories of mental illness, according to the ancient Greeks, with symptoms of inactivity and extreme depression.
pharmacist   Someone who prepares and sells drugs.
phlegm   A slimy liquid made in the lungs.
plague   In ancient Greece, a plague was any terrible disease that affected many people. Later the word would come to mean a specific disease: bubonic plague.
pleurisy   A condition in which part of the lung becomes swollen, breathing is difficult, and fever develops.
pneumonia   A lung disease.
prickly heat   The appearance of itchy spots on the body following swelling of the sweat glands, usually occurring in very hot weather.
prognosis   A mixture of diagnosis (identifying a disease) and predicting how the disease will progress.
psoriasis   A skin disease that causes sore red patches covered with white scales.
root cutter   Someone who collected plants to be used to make medicines.
smallpox   A serious virus that covered the body with itchy, pus-filled red bumps and was often fatal.
tonsillitis   A condition in which tissues in the throat called tonsils become swollen.
tuberculosis   Also known as consumption. A disease that affects the lungs.
typhus   A disease that can be fatal, causing high fever, terrible headaches, and a dark red rash.
vivisection   Cutting open a live animal body in order to examine its parts.

Further Information

Further Reading

Chisholm, Jane. *The Usborne Internet-Linked Encyclopedia of Ancient Greece.* New York: Usborne, 2002.

Dawson, Ian. *Greek and Roman Medicine.* New York: Enchanted Lion Books, 2005.

Doak, Robin S. *Thucydides: Ancient Greek Historian.* Minneapolis: Compass Point Books, 2007.

Lassieur, Allison. *The Ancient Greeks.* New York: Franklin Watts, 2004.

Nardo, Don. *World History: Greek and Roman Science.* San Diego: Lucent Books, 1998.

Pearson, Anne. *Ancient Greece.* New York: Dorling Kindersley, 2004.

On the Web

For more information on this topic, use FactHound.
1. Go to *www.facthound.com*
2. Type in this book ID: 0756520878
3. Click on the *Fetch It* button.

FactHound will find the best Web sites for you.

Index

anatomy 11, 30
anesthetics 18, 19
Apollo 6, 8
Aretaeus 28, 29
asklepieion 8
Asklepios 5, 9, 12, 17, 26
Athens 4, 12, 24, 25

babies 12, 21, 22
baths 17, 20
bedside manner 14
blood 8, 10, 11, 26
bloodletting 10, 27

Celsus, Cornelius 11, 18
childbirth 22–23
colds and flu 13, 20

depression 19, 28, 29
diagnoses 16–17
diet 9, 17, 18, 20
Dionysus 28, 29
Dioscorides 19
disease 5, 6, 7, 8, 10, 12, 13, 14,
   16, 17, 18, 20, 24, 25
dissection 11
doctors 5, 14–15, 16, 18, 19
dreams 9, 16
drugs 17, 18–19

epidemics 24–25
epilepsy 12, 13
exercise 9, 17, 20, 21

fever 10, 19, 24

gods 5, 6, 7, 8, 9, 10, 18, 28, 29

heart 8, 11, 20
herbalists 18, 19
herbal remedies 8, 9, 18–19
herbals 18
herbs 18, 19, 22, 26
Herophilus 18, 23
Hesiod 6, 7
Hippocrates 5, 10, 12, 13, 14, 15,
   17, 22, 25, 27, 28
Hippocratic oath 14
Homer 6, 8, 20, 26
humors 10, 16, 28
hunting 21
Hygeia 8, 9

mandrake 19
mania 28, 29
Marcellus 18
massage 17, 20
medicine 5, 8, 10, 18, 26
mental illness 13, 28–29
midwives 23
myths 6, 7

natural healing 17

old age 12, 21

Panacea 8
Pandora's box 7
pharmacists 14
plague 6, 7, 24
plants 18, 19
Plato 10, 18
pneumonia 12, 13
pregnancy 21, 22
priests 8, 9, 26
prognosis 17

root cutters 18

sacrifices 8
shrines 9, 26, 30
Sparta 4, 21, 22, 24
sports 20, 21
surgeons 14, 26, 27
surgery 9, 26–27
surgical tools 27
symptoms 17

Theophrastus 16
Thucydides 24
tuberculosis 13, 18

vivisection 11
votive reliefs 9, 12

women 21, 22, 23
wounds 8, 26

Xenophon 21

Zeus 6, 7, 28

DATE DUE

WITHDRAWN